Dropshipping

How To Make Make Money Online And Build Your Own $100,000+ Dropshipping Online Business

Anthony Parker

ISBN: 1979374600
ISBN-13: 9781979374606

TABLE OF CONTENTS

Introduction

Thank you for taking the time to purcase this book: Dropshipping: How To Make Money Online And Build Your Own $100,000+ Dropshipping Online Business.

This book covers the topic of dropshipping and will teach you everything you need to know about building a successful dropshipping business.

At the completion of this book, you will have a good understanding of what it takes to build a dropshipping online business and be able to start your own $100,000+ dropshipping business from scratch.

Once again, thanks for purchasing this book, I hope you find it to be helpful!.

Chapter One: Introduction To Dropshipping

In recent years, the dropshipping business model has taken the ecommerce world by storm. While estimates vary, industry watchers have discovered that close to 30 percent of online retailers use the dropshipping model. This shows that dropshipping is a proven business model that anyone can achieve success with. If done correctly, dropshipping is a great business option because it gives you the ability to make money passively. In other words, you will be able to make money with very little effort. While this sounds easy, you need to know the ins and outs of dropshipping in order to achieve success. Before we delve into the principles that will set you up for success, let's start by understanding what drop shipping is.

What Is Dropshipping?

Dropshipping is a business model where a business sells products without having to keep them in stock. Instead, when a customer orders a product, the dropshipping merchant transfers the order to a third party, who then ships the product directly to the customer. This means that the dropshipping merchant does not see or handle the product. The main difference between a dropshipping merchant and a standard retailer is that the dropshipping merchant does not own any of the stock they are selling. Instead, they purchase the inventory from a third party as needed—only when a customer has made an order.

The Advantages Of Dropshipping

Low Capital Requirements

This is probably the biggest advantage of dropshipping. Since one does not need to purchase any inventory, they can launch an ecommerce store with minimal capital. The dropshipping merchant only purchases a product after it has been paid for by the customer, which means they need very little money to start their dropshipping business. The only capital needed to start a dropshipping business is the money required to develop your online store. If you are a skilled web developer, the capital requirements become even lower. Compare this to traditional retailers, who have to spend thousands of dollars to stock their stores with inventory.

Much Easier To Start And Operate

When compared to a traditional retail business, a dropshipping business is a lot easier to start and operate, mainly because you don't have the hassle of dealing with the actual physical products. As a dropshipping entrepreneur, you don't have to worry about leasing and managing a warehouse, packing and shipping customer orders, keeping track of your inventory, or managing stock levels and handling returns. You only need to concentrate on finding customers for your business and ensuring orders are fulfilled.

Scalability

With a traditional retail business, if business increases threefold, you will need to do a lot of extra work to keep up with the extra customers. You might need to hire more employees or find more capital to increase your inventory. With a dropshipping business, if there is an increase in the number of orders, most of the extra work will be borne by your dropshipping suppliers. This means that you can easily grow your business without increasing your overhead costs or having to do more work.

Ideal For Newcomers

Setting up a dropshipping business is really simple, even for people who do not have any previous experience with internet marketing and ecommerce. Since the suppliers handle most of the stressful parts of the business, you will have enough time to learn how to manage your dropshipping business.

Low Overheads

Since dropshipping merchants do not deal directly with physical products, they don't have the costs associated with purchasing stock or managing a warehouse. They only pay for stock after they have been paid for it, which eliminates the risk of buying stock that no one will buy. All this means that their overhead expenses are usually very low. Actually, it is possible to run a successful dropshipping business from home with just a laptop and a monthly budget of under $100. As your business grows, these expenses might increase. However, they will still be quite low compared to running a traditional retail business.

Flexibility And Freedom

This is a major allure of the dropshipping business model. Since you don't have a brick-and-mortar store or warehouse, you can run your dropshipping business from anywhere in the world. All you need is an internet connection and the ability to communicate with your customers and suppliers. This gives dropshipping entrepreneurs the flexibility to choose their own working schedules and the freedom and independence of living the lifestyle of their dreams.

Wide Product Selection

Since you don't have to pre-purchase the products you sell in your dropshipping store, you don't have any limits to the array of products you can offer. If you want to expand your assortment, simply find a supplier who stocks the items and then put the items up for sale on your ecommerce store. You can do this at no extra cost.

Wide Market

Since your dropshipping business is based online, it means you are not limited by geographical boundaries. You can sell to people from any part of the world, so long as they have an internet connection.

With all these advantages, you can see why dropshipping is such an attractive business model for both beginners and established merchants. However, this does not mean that running a dropshipping business is a bed of roses. Dropshipping has its disadvantages as well.

The Disadvantages Of Dropshipping

Narrow Margins

This is one of the biggest disadvantages of a dropshipping business, especially if you are selling products in a highly competitive niche. Since starting a dropshipping business is easy and the overhead expenses are so low, many people will start a dropshipping business and sell their products at very low prices in an attempt to entice customers. With the low capital investments, they don't really feel a pinch even when they operate at such narrow margins.

While you might have invested in a high-quality website and excellent customer care, prospective customers can quickly compare your prices to those of your competitors who don't care about having high margins. This means that if you are not careful, you can easily find yourself competing on price, which will drive your profit margins even lower. To avoid getting into this rut, you should select a good niche that is better suited for a dropshipping business. I will discuss this in detail in Chapter Three.

Inventory Management Issues

With a traditional retail business, you stock your own items, so it is fairly easy to keep track of products that are in stock and those that are out of stock. However, as a dropshipping merchant, you have to source your products from multiple suppliers, who are also supplying other dropshipping merchants. This means that their inventories change on a day-to-day and sometimes hourly basis. There are solutions that allow you to sync your inventory with your suppliers', but they don't always work as expected. In such situations, a customer might end up paying for a product that has run out of stock from your supplier. This might cause you a lot of headaches as you try to find new suppliers to fulfill the order.

Shipping Complexities

As a dropshipping entrepreneur, you will most likely work with multiple suppliers. This means that different products on your ecommerce store will be sourced from different suppliers, which might end up complicating your shipping costs. For instance, a customer might order four different products from your ecommerce store. If these four products are sourced from different suppliers, you will need to pay the shipping charges for each item separately. However, charging the customer a separate shipping fee for each item might not be a very wise decision, so you will end up covering part of their shipping costs. Even if you were to charge the customer the different shipping costs for each item, automating these calculations on your business website can be quite a challenge.

Supplier Errors

Most suppliers will be handling lots of orders, not only from you, but from other dropshipping merchants. It is inevitable that they are going to make some errors and bungle some orders. However, you will have to take accountability for the mistakes and apologize to your customers. Remember, your customers are dealing with you and not the supplier. Therefore, it is your business's reputation that is on the line. To minimize this, you should avoid mediocre suppliers, since they will only cause you endless frustration. I will discuss how to choose a great supplier in Chapter Four.

Chapter Summary

In this chapter, you have discovered:

- What dropshipping is.
- The benefits of dropshipping.
- The disadvantages of dropshipping.

In the next chapter, you are going to learn about the dropshipping order fulfillment process.

Chapter Two: The Dropshipping Order Fulfillment Process

In this chapter, I am going to look at the dropshipping supply chain. This is the process that the product follows from the moment it is manufactured to the moment it gets to the customer. For this, we need to first take a look at the three most important players that are involved in the dropshipping supply chain.

Manufacturers: These are the companies that create the products. In most cases, manufacturers do not sell directly to consumers. Instead, they sell to wholesalers and retailers, who buy in bulk. When you want to resell a product, buying from a manufacturer is the cheapest option. However, most manufacturers have minimum purchase requirements, which means that you cannot buy below a certain quantity of product. This means that you have to stock the products yourself and re-ship to your customers when they order. For this reason, buying directly from manufacturers is not a very good option when your aim is to run a dropshipping business.

Wholesalers: These companies buy the products from the manufacturers in bulk and then sell them to retailers at a slight markup. While wholesalers might also have a minimum purchase requirement, theirs is usually much lower when compared to that of the manufacturers. In most cases, wholesalers will have products from many different manufacturers. Some wholesalers sell strictly to retailers, while others sell to consumers as well. As a dropshipping merchant, the best option is to source your products from a wholesaler.

Retailers: This is any business that directly sells products to consumers. If you run a dropshipping business, you fall into this category.

You might be surprised that "dropshipper" does not appear on the list of players involved in the dropshipping supply chain. The reason is because dropshipping is not a role. Instead, it is a service. This means that any of the above players can act as a dropshipper or dropshipping supplier. It is possible to find manufacturers who are willing to dropship their products directly to your customers. Similarly, it is possible to find a retailer who is willing to ship directly to your customers. However, their prices are not going to be as competitive as those of a manufacturer or wholesaler.

Why is this information important? This information is meant to teach you to perform due diligence when searching for a supplier. While many companies might claim to be dropshipping suppliers, it does not mean that they are giving you their products at wholesale prices. It only means that they are willing to handle the shipping on your behalf. To be sure that you are getting the best possible price, you should ensure that your supplier is a legitimate manufacturer or wholesaler. I am going to discuss the process of choosing a supplier in greater detail in Chapter Four.

The Order Fulfillment Process

Now that you know the major players involved in the dropshipping supply chain, we are going to take a look at the dropshipping order fulfillment process, from the moment the customer makes the order on your website to the moment the product gets delivered to them. To make it easier for you to understand, we are going to follow an order placed on TV World, a theoretical dropshipping store that deals in TV sales. We are going to assume that TV World sources its products from a supplier we'll call Universal TV Wholesalers.

The entire process might go like this:

Step 1: Customer places order with TV World.

Mr. Oscar needs to buy a TV for his living room. He comes across the TV World ecommerce store, where he finds a TV that he likes and places an order. When his order gets approved, the following things take place:

- Mr. Oscar's payment is captured and automatically deposited into TV World's bank account.
- The ecommerce store generates an email confirmation of the new order, which is sent to both Mr. Oscar and TV World.

Step 2: TV World places an identical order with Universal TV Wholesalers.

TV World forwards the email confirmation message to Universal TV Wholesalers. Since they have a dropshipping arrangement in place, Universal TV Wholesalers already has TV World's credit card information. Universal TV Wholesalers bills the wholesale price, as well as the shipping charges (plus any other processing fees) to TV World's credit card.

It's important to note that some dropshipping suppliers have sophisticated systems that allow the ecommerce store to automatically upload orders. However, email remains the easiest and most common way for the ecommerce store owner to place orders with the dropshipping supplier.

Step 3: Universal TV Wholesalers Ships the Order

If Universal TV Wholesalers has the ordered TV in stock and was able to successfully bill TV World the wholesale price of the TV, they will then package the TV and ship it directly to Mr. Oscar's address. It's important to note that though the TV was sent by Universal TV Wholesalers, the package will have TV World's name and address on the return address. The invoice and packing slip will also bear TV World's name and logo. Universal TV

Wholesalers also sends an invoice and the tracking number to TV World.

Another important thing to note is that most high quality dropshipping suppliers have a fast turnaround time. This allows the ecommerce store owner to advertise same-day shipping, even though they are sourcing the product from a third-party supplier.

Step 4: TV World alerts Mr. Oscar of the shipment.

After receiving the tracking number from Universal TV Wholesalers, TV World will then forward it to Mr. Oscar. With this, the order fulfillment process is completed. The product has been shipped to the customer, the payment has been collected, the supplier has been paid, and the customer has been notified that his product is on its way. The difference between what Mr. Oscar paid and what was paid to Universal TV Wholesalers is TV World's profit.

One thing becomes very clear about this process: In spite of playing a very crucial role in the whole process, the dropshipping supplier remains completely invisible to the customer. Since the package bears TV World's name and return address, the customer will contact TV World in case he receives the wrong order or in case the product is faulty. TV World will then make behind-the-scene arrangements to make sure Universal TV Wholesalers sends the right product. Mr. Oscar has no way of knowing that a third party was involved in fulfilling his order, since the marketing, payment processing, and customer service was all done by TV World.

Chapter Summary

In this chapter, you have learned:

- The key players involved in the dropshipping order fulfillment process.
- How the dropshipping order fulfillment process works.

In the next chapter, we will explore the process of picking a niche and product to sell on your dropshipping store.

Chapter Three: Niche And Product Selection

When starting your own dropshipping business, one of the earliest challenges you are going to face is selecting which niche and products you are going to focus on. This is one of the biggest decisions you will be required to make and it is going to have a big impact on your chances of success.

One of the most common mistakes that new dropshipping entrepreneurs make at this point is picking a niche just because they are personally interested in it. Sure, you may have heard before that you should create a business around something about which you are passionate. While this will make things easier for you, it doesn't guarantee success. If anything, it might contribute to your business's failure. Remember, you are starting a business with the aim of making profit. Therefore, you should put your personal interests aside and do proper market research to ensure that you have a niche that is going to sell.

Another common mistake with new dropshippers is trying to pick a niche that is too broad. It's easy to understand why they do this. After all, if your niche is broad, you have access to a huge market and you can sell a wide variety of products, right? However, your chances of success with a broad niche are very low. It will be a tough task getting traffic to such a dropshipping store.

To increase your chances of success, you should focus on a narrow niche. Some benefits of narrowing down your niche selection include:

- It will be easier for you to get a better understanding of that niche and therefore position yourself as an expert.
- It is a lot easier to rank your store higher in search engines for specific search queries instead of trying to rank for dozens of search terms.
- It is always easier to dominate a small niche compared to a broad niche. This will in turn build your credibility.
- There's less competition in a narrower niche.

- Since you offer specialized products, customers will come back to your store because you are the one in their minds when they think of products in your particular niche.

- Focusing on one specific audience makes it easier for you to plan your marketing strategies.

Factors That Contribute To Ecommerce Success

There are a few things which lead to a high chance of success for businesses that sell products online. To be successful, you should do one of the following:

- **Have your own product**: If you produce your own product, you control the supply and distribution of the product. You have virtually no competition and you can charge a premium price for the product. While this almost always guarantees success, it is not an option when you want to start a dropshipping business, since dropshipping requires you to sell products manufactured by other people.

- **Gain access to exclusive pricing or distribution**: This is another way that almost guarantees success when selling online. If you can make arrangements with a manufacturer to be the exclusive distributor of their product—or have access to exclusive pricing—you can build a successful business selling online. The problem is, getting access to such arrangements is not easy. As a dropshipper, you will likely use a supplier who offers the same products and wholesale prices to several other dropshipping merchants.

- **Sell at the most competitive prices**: If it is possible for you to offer the most competitive prices, you can easily attract a large portion of the market. Unfortunately, this is not a very wise business model. If your only advantage as a dropshipping merchant is a low price, you will soon find yourself in a price war that will bring down your margins and drive you out of business. You simply can't compete with ecommerce giants like Amazon on price.

- **Add non-price value to your products**: As a dropshipping entrepreneur, this is the best way to set your business apart from the competition and build your dropshipping business for success. It also allows you to charge a premium price for your products, which people will easily pay because of the additional value they are getting from your business. When shopping for products online, people often face a few things that hamper their buying experience. If you can solve these challenges for them, then you have found a way to differentiate yourself from the competition.

As a dropshipping entrepreneur, there are several ways you can add non-price value to your products. Provide your customers with expert advice and guidance on challenging issues around your niche. Create comprehensive buyer's guides that help your customers make the best buying decisions. Ensure your products are accompanied by high-quality product images that give your customers a good sense of the products you are selling. Take the time to come up with detailed product descriptions that give your customers an honest look into the products. Invest in comprehensive setup and installation guides and create high-quality videos that show your customers how to use the products. If your products have accompanying accessories, create in-depth guides that help you customers understand component compatibility. Invest in having a quality customer service for your ecommerce store. There are many more ways of adding non-price value to your products. You simply have to make it easier for your customers to understand and use whatever you are selling. It's also good to note that some niches and products are more suited to this strategy than others.

Targeting The Best Customers

Even before you go to product selection, you need to make sure that you are targeting the right customer demographic. Have you ever noticed how some customers will pay thousands of dollars for a product without flinching, while others will only pay a couple bucks and feel entitled to a king's treatment? Targeting a demographic that has no qualms spending on whatever product you are selling is a surefire way of increasing your chances of success as a dropshipper. When building your dropshipping business, you should target one of these three customer categories:

- **Businesses**: While businesses will be looking for a good deal when it comes to price, they usually order products in large quantities. Businesses also tend to buy their supplies from the same merchant. Once you build rapport with business clients and earn their trust, chances are you will have earned yourself long-term, high-volume clients. The best bet is to go for products that appeal to both business clients and individual customers.

- **Hobbyists**: This is a highly profitable customer category since most people are so passionate about their hobbies that they are willing to spend insane amounts of money to get tools and equipment related to their hobbies. Serious gamers will invest thousands of dollars to ensure that they have the perfect gaming rig. Serious mountain bikers will spend more on their bikes than their cars. From this, it's evident that if you target the right hobbyist niche, you can easily make a fortune.

- **Repeat buyers**: The beauty of repeat buyers is that they provide you with recurring revenue. By selling products that have to be replaced frequently, you can easily build a profitable business with loyal customers who will return to you every time they need to replace their product. The best part is that repeat buyers have a higher customer lifetime value. Instead of having to find new customers every time, you only need to find a customer once and they will keep buying from you for years to come.

Identifying Great Dropshipping Products

Once you have identified the customer demographic you want to target from the three categories discussed above, the next step is identifying what product you will actually sell to them. Even if you target the right demographic, you will greatly curtail your chances of success if you pick the wrong product to sell.

This doesn't mean that there is a perfect dropshipping product. Most beginners get caught up in analysis paralysis as they try to find a perfect product. In the end, they get overwhelmed by this search for an elusive "perfect product" and give up altogether. While there is no perfect product, there is a set of criteria you can use to evaluate your product idea and see if it's worth it. If you have a list of ideas, you simply need to check them against this set of criteria to find products that have a high chance of success. The factors you need to keep in mind when evaluating your product ideas are:

Price

When it comes to dropshipping, price is a double-edged sword. If you sell low-priced products, you are likely to make a lot of sales. This means that you will have more chances of getting customer feedback, which is crucial for the success of your dropshipping business. However, your profit per product will be low. If you sell high-priced products, you will have high profits, but you are unlikely to make as many sales.

You also need to consider the buyer's psychology. Most people will comfortably order a $200 product online without having to talk to anyone on the phone. However, if you are selling a $2,000 item, people will need to speak to a representative to make sure that the whatever they are buying is the right fit for them and that the store is not a fraud. This means that if you want to sell highly-priced products, you should invest in personalized phone support which will be crucial in ensuring that customers buy. You will also need to ensure that your margins are able to cover the extra support you are offering.

While there is no perfect price, either, the $100 to $500 range seems to be a sweet spot for dropshipping products. People will comfortably spend on products within this price range without requiring a lot of pre-sale support. At the same time, this price range allows you to make a healthy profit. Ideally, I would advise you to aim for a 20 – 40% margin. Depending on your niche and the products you are selling, it is even possible to have 100% margins.

Another thing you should consider when it comes to pricing is to find products with a minimum advertised price (MAP) or a minimum retail price (MRP). These are products where the manufacturer sets a floor price for all their resellers. This means that resellers cannot sell the products below this price. Products with a MAP or MRP are good for dropshipping because they prevent you from having to compete on price. This allows you to strengthen the quality of your service without having to worry that you will lose business to cheaper but less reputable merchants.

Generic Brands

What kind of cell phone are you currently using? If you were to buy another one, would you buy the same brand? Chances are if you use an iPhone, you would buy another iPhone. If you own a Samsung TV, chances are you would buy a Samsung TV. This is because of something known as brand loyalty. When choosing the products to sell on your dropshipping business, you should avoid product categories which have already established customer loyalty. There's little you can do to convince these customers to buy your products. Moreover, if you are selling a Samsung TV, Best Buy is selling the same TV, probably at a more competitive price than you.

When you are looking for a dropshipping product, you should go for products that do not have any established brands. This means that the customer does not know which brand they should go for and are therefore comfortable buying from any manufacturer. To make this easier to grasp, I will use an illustration. Let's say I live in a coastal town and I become interested in surfing. I know that I need to get myself a surfboard. However, having no prior knowledge of surfing, so I don't know which brand makes the best surfboards. When I go online to shop for a surfboard, I don't care which company made the surfboard, as long as the surfboard is within my budget and has some good reviews online.

To give another example, let's assume that Prudence is giving her living room a new look and needs to get some new curtains. She knows the kind of curtains she wants, but she can't seem to find them at her local departmental store. So, she searches for the curtains online. She comes across a website that has the exact kind of curtains she wants. Prudence does not care who made the curtains, so long as they please her and are within her budget.

Likewise, you should go for products that have no established brands, which means that customers will buy your products as long as they meet their expectations.

Multiple Accessories

Selling a product that requires multiple accessories is a great way of increasing your average sale size, as well as your overall margin. For instance, if you sell a digital camera, the customer might need to buy batteries and a memory stick, as well. Apart from increasing the sale size, products with multiple accessories have another advantage. When it comes to retail, you will find that lower-priced accessories usually have higher margins compared to higher-priced items.

For instance, a store selling a one-thousand-dollar computer might only make a 10% profit on the computer. However, the customer might also buy a keyboard, an HDMI cable, a webcam, and a mouse. While these items might be very low in price compared to the computer, the store might earn a 100% or more margin on these low-ticket items. This might not seem like much, but let's take a closer look at it. While the store made a $100 profit on the computer, they probably made $10 of the $20 mouse, $30 on a $40 keyboard and another $30 on a $50 webcam. The profits from these smaller sales can quickly add up and bypass the high-ticket item.

A customer who bought a thousand-dollar computer is also less likely to care about the price of a $20 mouse. Instead of having to shop around for a cheaper mouse, they will probably just buy it from the same store where they bought the computer. To take advantage of this, some merchants set a very low price for the main item (without making a profit), with the hope that this will attract customers who will then buy multiple accessories as well.

Another advantage of selling products with multiple accessories is that it provides you the opportunity to add non-price value to the products. If the product requires multiple components to work properly, this is an opportunity for you to offer your advice on the accessories that work best with the product and sell them to your customers.

Small And Lightweight

Smaller and lighter products are usually more affordable to ship, which means that it will be easier for you to make higher profit margins, especially if you are offering free shipping. While there's potential to make insane profits on some big, heavy products, I would recommend that you keep away from these as a beginner. You can venture into them after gaining some experience running a dropshipping business.

Hard To Find Locally

Your chances of success selling online—both as a dropshipping merchant or a standard online retailer—are higher if you sell products that are hard to find locally. If your products can be found at the neighborhood store, why would anyone buy them from your site? For instance, looking at our earlier example, if Prudence had found the curtains she was looking for at her local store, she wouldn't have gone online.

Products That Are Customizable Or Confusing/Hard To Install Or Set Up

Customizable and confusing products are a great choice for dropshipping. If a product is customizable or confusing, people will need information to help them understand how to use or customize it. You can leverage this knowledge gap to create premium content—guides and videos—that helps you set your business apart from the competition while also helping your customers understand your products. This content also gives you the leverage to charge higher prices for your products.

This also holds true for products that are difficult to set up or install. If your product comes with a detailed video guide that will help your customer install it easily and in a short time, there's a high chance that the customer will buy it from you, despite the product being available elsewhere for a couple dollars less.

Low Turnover

By now, you know that investing in a high-quality website with premium, helpful content is something you should do for your dropshipping business. However, if you are selling products that change or get upgraded each year, you will need to update your website every time the new products hit the market. This is both time consuming and expensive. To avoid this, you should go for products that don't get upgraded after every short while. This will allow you to reap more from the time and money invested in your website.

Disposable Or Renewable Products

Remember how I mentioned that selling to repeat buyers is a good approach? Well, disposable and renewable products are the source of repeat buyers. If your products need to be renewed every so often, customers will keep coming to your site every time the need to renew the product. To take advantage of renewable products, you can offer your customers a subscription service. This makes it convenient for them and guarantees you a recurring income stream. You can offer discounts to incentivize customers to sign up for the subscription service.

How To Measure Demand For Your Product And Niche

By now, you should have decided on a number of products you would like to focus on by comparing them against the factors discussed above. The next step is to find out if there is any demand for your preferred products. This step is very important. It doesn't matter if your product matches all the criteria discussed above; if people don't want your product, you are not going to make any money. It is a lot easier to sell products when there is existing demand than to try and create new demand for a product.

The good thing is that there are a ton of online tools you can use to evaluate demand for your products. In this part, I will take you through the process of using some of these tools to evaluate demand for your chosen products.

Google Keyword Tool

This is the most well-known and the most popular tool for measuring demand for a product or niche. This tool allows you to measure the online demand for a product by finding out the number of people who are actively searching for the product on the Google search engine. To find how many people are searching for a product, simply type the keyword or phrase that defines the product on the Google keyword tool and it will show you the number of people searching for that word or phrase each month.

However, the Google keyword tool is a lot more extensive than this. There's a ton of data that you can uncover with it. I won't go into an in-depth review of this tool as that would require an entire book of its own. I will instead highlight three things that you should always keep in mind when performing your searches if you want to get the most out of this tool.

Match Type: When searching for keywords, the tool allows you to select between three match types—broad, phrase, or exact match. For the most accurate picture of the number of people searching for your product of choice, you should select the exact match option, unless you have a good reason that requires you to use a different option.

Search Location: The Google keyword tool also gives search volumes based on geographical location. When you perform your search, ensure that you have distinguished between local and global search volumes. If your intention is sell products in a specific region, your focus should be on the local search volume. If a product has a high global search volume but a very low volume in the region where you intend to sell, you should either change the product or rethink your target market.

Long-Tail Variations: When looking at the search volumes for a product, you should go beyond the broad keywords, since they might mislead you. While these broad keywords might show a high search volume, your search traffic will mostly come from longer, more specific search queries, which are known as long-tail search queries. These long-tail search queries might have a significantly lower search volume than the broad keywords, but they are more important. For instance, if you find that a broad keyword is accompanied by long-tail variations which also have a high search volume, it shows that there is a lot of interest and variety in that particular product or niche. However, if you find that the broad keywords have high search volumes, but there's little long-tail search volume after the high-level keywords, you should be wary about selling these products or entering the niche.

Google Trends

While the Google keyword tool is a good way of discovering the raw search figures, Google Trends offers a better way for you to uncover more detailed market insights. Some of the information you want to look at using Google Trends includes:

Search volume over time: This allows you to see whether the search volume for a given search query has been growing or declining over time. This is important since you want to know whether the niche you want to get into is growing or declining. A declining search volume should act as a red flag that the niche is dying.

Top and rising terms: Apart from the performance of your search keywords over time, Google Trends also allows you to see the most popular searches related to your keywords, as well as the queries which have recently had a sharp increase in popularity. Analyzing popular and fast-growing terms is important because it will help you plan your marketing campaign and SEO efforts.

Geographical concentration: This is another important feature that allows you to see the geographical areas where there's a lot of people searching for a specific term. This helps you find out the geographical regions with a high customer base concentration for a specific niche. This tells you the geographic regions where you need to focus your marketing efforts. As a dropshipping entrepreneur, it also helps you choose the best suppliers to partner with, since you want suppliers that are close enough to most of your customers.

Seasonality: Google Trends also helps you understand the seasonality of the niche you are interested in. Does the demand for your product have significant changes during different times of the year? Remember, the keyword tool only provides average monthly searches. This can mislead you into thinking that there is demand for a product all year round. However, with Google Trends, you will be able to identify if you should expect demand for the product to fluctuate during the year. For instance, a product might have high demand in some months and virtually no demand in other months. If you had only looked at the average monthly search volume, you would have ended up overestimating the demand size for the product.

How To Measure Competition For Your Niche

The amount of competition is another delicate factor to consider before choosing a niche for your dropshipping business. You don't want too much competition, but you don't want zero competition either. Too much competition in a niche is not a good thing because you will most likely be in competition with established businesses with huge budgets and manpower. Building traffic to your dropshipping store will also be more difficult when there is too much competition. On the other hand, too little competition might mean that the market for that particular niche is not too large, which will in turn curtail your ability to grow.

While there are some dropshipping businesses that depend on paid advertising to drive traffic, most of them rely on free search traffic. This means that the easiest way of measuring the amount of competition in a specific niche is to evaluate the top dropshipping stores that rank organically (not paid) on Google's first page for a specific search query. This is because you have to compete against and outrank these sites in order to drive a significant level of traffic to your dropshipping store.

There are several factors that contribute to a website's ranking on Google. I will not go into a detailed discussion of these factors, but I will discuss four metrics which you can use to easily evaluate the competition and get a feel for the strength of your competition and what it will take to outrank them and drive traffic to your dropshipping store.

Linking Domains

One of the most important factors Google's search engine algorithm relies on to rank sites are backlinks. Keeping other factors constant, the more sites that link to a given website, the higher the website will be ranked. If you know the number of backlinks a competing dropshipping store has, then you have an idea of the number of backlinks you need to build to your website in order to outrank them.

While several different SEO metrics may be used to evaluate a website's ranking strength, there is one metric which is gives a fairly accurate measure. This metric is known as "unique linking domains" or "linking root domain." This metric refers to the number of backlinks a site has from unique domains. If there are several backlinks originating from the same domain, this metric only counts them as one, since they are all from the same domain.

To make it better for you to understand how this metric works, I will use an illustration. If a good friend recommends a certain movie, you might remember it or forget all about it. If your friend keeps talking about how great the movie was each day of the week (totaling seven recommendations from him), chances are you might be moved to watch the movie. However, if seven different friends recommend the movie, you are definitely going to check out the movie. In this case, the recommendations of the seven different friends hold more authority than the seven recommendations from one friend. This is how linking root domain works. Instead of counting different backlinks from the same domain as different repeatedly, it counts them as one unique backlink. Just like you, Google's ranking algorithm places higher importance on links from different sites. This means that while a site might have 50 backlinks, if they are all from just three sites, it is not as strong as a site with 10 backlinks from different sites.

There are several tools available online that you can use to find a site's linking root domain metric. When evaluating your competitors using linking root domain, you should analyze the metrics for the first, second, and third sites on Google search results, as well as the metrics for the last site on page one of Google search results. This helps give you an idea of what you need to do get onto the first page, as well as how to rank as the top site on Google's search results for your search query. Most internet users will open one of the sites that is among the top 10 on the search results, so for starters, you should know what it will take to get ranked in the first page.

Competition Site Authority

Like I mentioned earlier, there are several factors that Google uses to rank a website. The number of backlinks is one factor.

Another equally important factor is the quality of the backlinks. This means that a link from a blog with 10 monthly readers will rank nowhere near a link from a site with a million readers per month. The more high authority sites that link to your site, the more important your site is perceived to be. Google uses a metric known as PageRank to measure a site's authority. Again, this metric alone won't give you an accurate evaluation of a site's authority, but it is a quick and easy way of evaluating the competition in a niche.

To evaluate your competition using PageRank, identify the top sites that rank for the specific search query you want to rank for and check the PageRank readings for their homepages. The higher the PageRank readings for a site, the higher the perceived authority of the site. If the top sites in a niche have a PageRank of 1 or 2, you can easily compete against and outrank them. However, this might mean that the market for this niche is relatively small.

If the top dropshipping sites in a niche have a PageRank of 3 to 4, it shows that the niche is fairly competitive. While outranking your competition in this range is not necessarily easy, it can still be done. A niche with such authority for the top dropshipping

41

sites is ideal for individual dropshipping entrepreneurs. A PageRank of 4 to 5 signifies sites with fairly high authority. To attain such an authority, your dropshipping store needs to have several backlinks from other authoritative domains, as well as several other regular links. If competitor sites in your niche have a PageRank of 6 or more, breaking into this niche will be outright difficult, unless you have a huge budget and manpower to dedicate to marketing and SEO. This might not be a good niche for an individual dropshipping entrepreneur.

Qualitative Metrics

While quantitative metrics like linking root domain and PageRank give a good evaluation of how hard it will be to compete against and outrank other players in your niche, you should not confine yourself to hard statistics only. You should also take a look at some qualitative factors, such as:

Site quality: Take a look at some of the top dropshipping sites in your chosen niche and assess them from a buyer's perspective. How does the design look and feel? How user friendly is the site? How is the site organized? How easy it to move around the site?

What kind of information is provided in regard to the listed products? How is the image quality?

If the top ecommerce sites in the niche provide an easy and high-quality shopping experience, it will be harder for you to break into the niche. However, if you see some areas where you can make some improvements, there is an opportunity for you to differentiate yourself by providing a better shopping experience.

Site reputation and customer loyalty: At times, your preferred niche may have some ecommerce stores that have been in existence for several years and have built a solid reputation. Some such sites might have an outdated site design, but it will still be hard to steal a chunk of the market from them. Similarly, some sites might have well-designed sites, but if they have an awful reputation, you can easily win over customers from them. To help you get a better understanding of a competitor's reputation, try searching for reviews on social media and other online forums. If you notice any point where a superior competitor does not meet customer expectations, then that is your opportunity to win these customers over by providing superior service.

When performing your competitor evaluation, it is important to realize that the results you see on Google are usually personalized based on a number of factors, such as browsing history and geographic location. This means that it is possible that your search might result in biased or skewed results. For instance, if you live in Europe but want to sell to customers in the United States, your results might display competitors in Europe, meaning you will still have no information about the actual competitors you will be facing.

To get the most accurate results, here are two methods you can use:

Incognito search: Browsers like Chrome allow you to surf the internet in "incognito" mode. In this mode, the browser does not track your history or location, which means you are more likely to get unbiased results when using this mode. Other browsers also have their own version of this "hidden" mode. Using these modes will increase your chances of getting results that are not skewed.

Searching for nation specific results: There are some text codes that you can use to refine your search results in Google.

This is what we will use to get nation-specific results. For instance, if you want to view US based results when you are not in the US, simply add "&gl=us" at the end of the URL on Google's search results page. Google has a guide on how to tweak their search engine for geo-targeted results, which you can use to find search results that are specific to different nations.

I would like to end this chapter with a disclaimer. There is no perfect dropshipping niche or product. The tips and strategies shared in this chapter will help you make a better decision and improve your chances of success, but there's no way to have a guarantee that your niche or product will totally work out. The only way to do this is to jump in and give it a try. The successful entrepreneurs are always those who will take action despite all the uncertainty that comes with starting a business.

Chapter Summary

In this chapter, we have explored:

- Factors that contribute to ecommerce success.
- How to target the best customers.
- How to identify great dropshipping products.
- How to measure demand for your niche.

- How to measure competition for your niche.

In the next chapter, we will cover the process of finding suitable suppliers for your dropshipping business.

Chapter Four: How To find Suppliers For Your Dropshipping Business

For new dropshipping entrepreneurs, the process of finding a reputable and reliable supplier for your dropshipping business can be daunting. There are a lot of "fake" dropshipping wholesalers, and if you are not careful, you might even end up being scammed. Unfortunately, many dropshipping wholesalers do not put a lot of focus on marketing and are therefore harder to find. This means that the "fake" wholesalers are more likely to appear frequently in your searches, hence the need for you to be more careful. In this chapter, I am going to show you how to go about the process of finding suitable suppliers for your dropshipping business.

Identifying "Fake" Dropshipping Wholesalers

Since it is clear that your chances of coming across non-genuine wholesalers in your searches are quite high, I will start by showing how to identify these "fake" wholesalers from a mile away. If you notice any of the following, it should act as a red flag that you are not dealing with a legitimate dropshipping wholesaler:

Ongoing Fees

Legitimate dropshipping wholesalers do not charge any ongoing fees so that you can do business with them. If you come across a dropshipping wholesaler who wants you to keep paying a monthly membership fee, there is a high possibility that they are not genuine. You should keep away from such suppliers.

However, it is important to note that there is a difference between suppliers and supplier directories. Supplier directories provide a list of legitimate wholesale suppliers, often organized by niche or product type. I will discuss supplier directories in more detail later in this chapter. It is not abnormal for a supplier directory to charge a onetime fee or a monthly charge. This does not mean that the directory is not genuine.

However, even when dealing with genuine dropshipping wholesalers, there are some legitimate fees you might be required to pay. These are:

Per-Order Fees: Do not confuse this with a pre-order fee. Normally, most wholesalers will charge a dropshipping fee for every order. These are typical fees and should not be cause for alarm. Per-order fees normally range between $2 - $5, depending on the size and nature of the product ordered. This charge is usually to cater for things like packaging, since it is costlier to pack and ship individual orders as compared to large orders.

Minimum Order Sizes: Most dropshipping wholesalers will have what is known as a minimum initial order size or a minimum order quantity (MOQ). This is the amount you are required to buy during your first order. The aim of doing this is to keep away window-shoppers who might ask lots of questions and generally waste the wholesaler's time and then leave without making any meaningful orders.

As a dropshipping entrepreneur, this might be a bit tricky for you. For instance, a supplier might have a $500 minimum initial order size, but the average order size on your dropshipping store is about $50. Should you pre-order $500 worth of products just to get your wholesaler account approved?

To navigate around this, you can opt to pre-pay the $500 to the supplier. The $500 shows that you are committed to meeting their minimum order size and acts as a credit against your dropshipping orders. This means that you have paid for the first $500 worth of products. Once you get an order, you will only need to pass it to your supplier without having to pay for it again, until your $500 is all used up.

The minimum order size is just a rule that is put in place to save the suppliers' time and ensure they get good business. Therefore, if you can, try and negotiate with them to reduce your minimum order quantity. If they think that you are serious and will bring good business, they might just lower the MOQ for you.

Selling Directly To The Public

Before getting into business with genuine dropshipping wholesalers, you have to go through an application process and prove that your business is legitimate. Without this, you cannot order from a dropshipping wholesaler. Therefore, if you find a supplier who sells products at "wholesale prices" to just anyone, that's just another retailer trying to dupe you into thinking you are getting a good deal.

How to Identify Good Suppliers

Now that you know how to identify a fake supplier, let's cross to the other side and look at the characteristics of a good supplier. Since suppliers are a critical element of your dropshipping business, you want to make sure you are not working with just any supplier. To build a reliable, trustworthy, and successful dropshipping business, you need to ensure you are working with the best suppliers you can find. Here are some characteristics you can use to identify top-notch suppliers:

Industry expertise: The sales representatives of great suppliers are knowledgeable about their industry and the products they carry. Knowledgeable representatives are important because in the first few days after launching your dropshipping store, you might need to reach out to them with some questions, especially if your business is in a niche you are not very familiar with.

Dedicated support: When running a new dropshipping business, you are definitely going to have some issues here and there. If you are dealing with a top-notch supplier, they will assign you a dedicated sales representative who will help you resolve any issues you might have. Without a dedicated support representative, your problems will usually take a long time to resolve, which will in turn hurt your business's reputation.

Good technology: A good supplier knows the benefits of having a system that is backed by good technology. It is easy to work with and makes it easier for you to automate your business. A system with good technology includes features such as comprehensive online catalogues, a real-time inventory management system, data feeds, and the ability to perform online searches for products.

One of the most important features you need to ascertain is whether your supplier supports an automatic data feed. This is a feature that continuously and automatically updates inventory data from the supplier. This data includes things like product photos, product names and descriptions, prices, and variants of the product.

Let's assume you stock 10 products which come in three different colors. This translates to 30 unique product listings. This means that you would have to update 25 product listings every time your supplier changes something. If you have a thousand products on your dropshipping store, making such an update would take you a lot of time. However, with an automatic data feed, the product listings get updated automatically whenever your supplier makes any changes on their end. This saves you a lot of time and allows you to concentrate on other aspects of your business, such as driving traffic to your store. Automatic feeds usually come in a CSV or XML file, though there are several different formats for delivering data feeds, depending on the system supported by your supplier.

Takes orders via email: While this does not sound like something very important, imagine having to call your supplier every time a customer places an order. This is tiring and more time-intensive. However, forwarding orders to your supplier via email is something that can be done easily, even if there are hundreds of orders.

Centrally located: This has to do with the time it takes to deliver orders. For instance, if you sell primarily to people in the United

States, with a centrally located supplier, most orders can be delivered within 2 to 3 business days. However, if a supplier is located on the west coast, for example, it can take up to a week for orders to be delivered to customers on the east coast. With a centrally located supplier, you can confidently promise your customers faster delivery times and pay lower shipping costs.

Organized and efficient: This has to do with the competency of the supplier and their staff. You don't want to work with a supplier who makes errors on every few orders, since this might ruin your business's reputation. Unfortunately, there is no accurate way of evaluating a supplier's efficiency and competency. The only way you can do this is by making a few test orders to the supplier. This will allow you to understand how fast they process orders and ship out products, how soon they send the invoice and product tracking information, the quality of their packaging, and so on.

How To Find Dropshipping Suppliers

Now that you know how to tell a quality supplier from a fake one, it's time to explore the actual process of finding a supplier for your dropshipping business. There are many different methods that you can use to find suppliers. Here, I will discuss some of the most popular and most effective methods of finding dropshipping suppliers.

Contact The Manufacturer

This is one of the best ways of finding legitimate wholesale suppliers. After deciding on the products you want to carry in your store, get in touch with the manufacturer of the products and ask them to give you a list of their authorized wholesale distributors. You can then call these distributors to find out if they dropship and inquire about their requirements for setting up a wholesaler account.

Most wholesale distributors deal in products from multiple manufactures in a specific niche, so this is a nice strategy for finding suppliers within a given niche. Another good thing is that after speaking to a couple of leading manufacturers in your niche, you will be able to identify the top wholesale distributors within that niche.

Good Old Google

In this day and age, you can use Google to find almost everything. This applies even in finding dropshipping suppliers. However, before you begin typing away on Google, there are a few things you need to keep in mind:

You will have to dig deep – Like I mentioned earlier, most wholesalers do not make a lot of effort when it comes to marketing and promotion. This means that you are probably not going to find your ideal dropshipping supplier on page one of Google. You might have to go deeper into the search results before finding a legitimate wholesaler with the characteristics we mentioned earlier.

You need to use modifiers – Since wholesalers are not spending a lot of time and effort on SEO to help you find their websites, you might have to try different variations of your search query before landing on the right wholesaler. Instead of just searching for "chandelier wholesalers" and leaving it at that, try other variations of the search terms, such as "chandelier suppliers," "chandelier distributors," etc. This way, you are more likely to turn up better results.

Don't be put off by the website – Just like they don't spend a lot of effort on marketing and SEO, wholesalers don't spend lots of time on website design either. It's not unusual to come across a high-quality wholesaler with a basic website that looks like it was designed a decade ago. While some suppliers may have well-designed sites, don't overlook a supplier because of the quality of their website.

Order From Competitors

If you can't seem to unearth any good suppliers on your own, you could always steal suppliers from your competitors. To do this, find an ecommerce store which also dropships their orders and place a small order with them. When your package arrives, Google the return address to find out the original place the package came from. There is a good chance that this will be a supplier's address.

Trade Shows

Attending trade shows is a great way of discovering major manufacturers and wholesalers in your niche and connecting with them. The beauty of trade shows is that they allow you to make contacts with suppliers and research viable products, all at the same time. To be able to do this, you need to have selected a niche already. If you have the money and the time to attend, trade shows are a great way of finding major suppliers you can partner with.

Supplier Directories

A supplier directory is simply a database that contains a list of suppliers. The suppliers are organized according to their niche, market, or product. One great advantage of supplier directories is that the suppliers have to pass some screening process before they can get listed. This means that all the suppliers you find in a directory are genuine. Some directories may demand charges before you can get access to their list of suppliers.

Paying for a supplier directory membership can be helpful, particularly when you are still trying to find ideas. However, if you are a cash strapped start up, you don't have to join a paid directory. If you have already decided on your niche and the products you want to sell, you can use the techniques I discussed earlier to find suppliers and save some cash. In addition, after you find suppliers and start your dropshipping business, you will hardly need to use the directory again, unless you decide to add new products or expand into a new niche.

All the same, supplier directories allow you to easily and quickly search for and discover suppliers in one spot. They are great for entrepreneurs who are still searching for ideas on which niches to enter or the products to carry in their dropshipping stores. If you have the money and need to find suppliers quickly, you should go ahead and pay for directory membership.

There are several supplier directories online, and I can't possibly discuss all of them here. However, I will highlight some of the most popular supplier directories:

Worldwide Brands: Established in 1999, Worldwide Brands is one of the pioneering supplier directories. It is widely known and lists thousands of wholesalers and over 10 million products. All the wholesalers listed on Worldwide Brands have to meet specific criteria to ensure that they are genuine, quality wholesalers. Worldwide Brands is a great place to brainstorm niche ideas and find genuine wholesalers. Unfortunately, some major suppliers are missing from the directory. Worldwide Brands charges $299 for lifetime access to their supplier database. For those who want lifetime access to thousands of suppliers and have no qualms about paying a large one-time fee, Worldwide Brands is a great option.

Doba: Established in 2002, Doba is a bit different from Worldwide Brands. Doba is more than a database of suppliers. It offers a centralized interface that integrates with dropshipping stores and allows them to place orders with multiple suppliers. Doha also has a Push-to-Market feature which allows you to automatically list products from its interface to marketplaces like eBay. Owing to its integration feature, Doba cannot handle thousands of suppliers. Instead, it has 165 legitimate suppliers and over 1.5 million products.

Doba charges a $60 monthly membership fee. While this might seem to be a bit on the high side, their centralized interface provides greater convenience than you will find with other directories. Doba is a great choice for dropshipping entrepreneurs who want the convenience of being able to order from multiple suppliers in one place. If their suppliers have the products you want, then it is definitely worth the cost. However, if you don't mind dealing with each supplier separately, you can use the other methods discussed to find your own suppliers and save yourself a significant amount of money.

SaleHoo: SaleHoo was established in 2005. It has a database of over 8,000 dropshipping suppliers and wholesalers. SaleHoo seems to be geared toward dropshipping merchants who sell their products on eBay and Amazon. SaleHoo has a membership fee of $67 per year, which is fair when you consider other directories' fees. They also offer a 60-day money back guarantee if you are not satisfied with their service. SaleHoo is a great choice if all you need is temporary access to a supplier directory.

Wholesale Central: Established in 1996, Wholesale Central is probably the oldest supplier directory. One unique thing about Wholesale Central is that it does not charge for access to its list of suppliers. You can browse and search for suppliers without paying a dime. Instead, suppliers pay Wholesale Central a fee to be listed in the directory. The suppliers on Wholesale Central are prescreened to ensure they are genuine and trustworthy. Wholesale Central has over 1,400 suppliers in its database and over 740,000 products.

Since viewing the suppliers on Wholesale Central is free, there is no reason why you should not give it a try. However, you need to be a little more careful when looking for suppliers on Wholesale Central. Some of the suppliers listed there are not really wholesalers, but rather retailers selling items at "wholesale" prices. You should be wary of such suppliers.

AliExpress

In recent years, there has been a lot of publicity about AliExpress and how it can help anyone create a dropshipping store at almost no cost. AliExpress is the sister site to Alibaba, a Chinese website that connects Western buyers to Chinese manufacturers. Unlike Alibaba, which is meant for wholesale purchases with minimum order quantity requirements, AliExpress is more suited to smaller purchases, which makes it ideal for dropshipping merchants. You can easily find suppliers on AliExpress, but you need to keep the following things in mind:

Don't immediately go for the lowest price: Don't get too excited when you find a supplier selling a product at a fraction of what other suppliers are selling it for. In some cases, the price of a product on AliExpress corresponds to its quality. This means that if you want high-quality products for your store, you should be careful about dropshipping suppliers who have extremely low prices. Remember, when the deal is too good, think twice.

When searching for suppliers on AliExpress, you will find that there are several suppliers who deal in similar goods. You should take the time to do a comparison of various suppliers and their prices. If you find that most suppliers have an average price for a certain product, yet one supplier has a significantly lower price for the same product, this might be a red flag that the product is of a lower quality. In such a case, you should check out the supplier's reviews to find out if any previous buyers have left negative reviews about the quality of the supplier's products—this is a great way of finding quality suppliers for your dropshipping store.

It's important to note that a lower price does not necessarily translate to poor quality products and vice versa. This leads me to my next point.

Look for suppliers with a 95+ positive feedback: When it comes to evaluating dropshipping suppliers from AliExpress, there are two important metrics that you should always keep in mind—the Feedback Score and the Positive Feedback Rate. The Feedback Score gives you a rough idea of the supplier's sales volume. The Positive Feedback Rate, on the other hand, is a representation of the percentage of the positive reviews a supplier has received. Generally, to avoid suppliers who cause you headaches by delivering low quality products or by not delivering at all, aim for suppliers with at least a 2,000 feedback score and a positive feedback rate of 95% or higher. Always have this in mind as you search for dropshipping suppliers on AliExpress.

When you are building your new dropshipping store, it is important to build a foundation of suppliers who can be trusted and relied on. While having a low feedback score does not mean that a supplier is not reliable, you don't want a trial and error process when it comes to suppliers. However, things change when it comes to the positive feedback rate. Look at individual product feedback and the number of times the supplier has sold the product. For instance, if a supplier has sold a product a thousand times and received a 90% positive feedback rate, it is safer to buy from this supplier as compared to one who has a 100% positive feedback rate but only two sales. Customer reviews are also a great way of evaluating a prospective supplier. Try to look for negative reviews since they are helpful when it comes to identifying any issues or defects the product might have.

If you come across a supplier who has the product you want but has yet to receive any feedback for the product, look at the other products sold by the same supplier and check their feedback. If the other products have positive reviews and feedback, there's a high chance that the product you want is also of good quality. However, if the client has negative reviews for the other products, you should probably stay away from them.

Be wary of suppliers carrying brand products: When searching for suppliers on AliExpress, you might come across some unscrupulous suppliers carrying counterfeit goods. You will hardly ever find genuine designer goods on AliEpxress. If you find a product bearing a popular brand name on the website, you should exercise caution because there's a likelihood that the product is a knock off. If you find that a supplier is stocking products that look counterfeited, you should avoid such a supplier because selling such products on your store could land you in legal trouble. Better yet, you should report such a seller to AliExpress.

Evaluate the supplier's responsiveness: Let's assume for a minute that an order has been delivered to a customer, but the customer is not satisfied for some reason. The customer demands that you reship the product and even goes ahead and files a dispute on your PayPal account. In such a situation, you need a dropshipping supplier who won't take ages to respond to you, right?

When you start running your own dropshipping store, you will find yourself in such situations. In order to keep yourself and your business safe during such times, you should gauge the responsiveness of a supplier before your start selling any of their products in your store. To gauge a supplier's responsiveness, simply write them a message and wait to see how long it takes them to give an appropriate response. Watch out how effectively they respond to your situation, as well. Doing this will save you a lot of trouble down the road.

Good dropshipping suppliers will give you a response quickly, take note of your problem, and try to resolve it as fast as they can. The good thing is that most suppliers on AliExpress are reliable.

Order samples to further evaluate a supplier: Despite having done all the preliminary research before settling on a specific supplier, the best way to ascertain the reliability and trustworthiness of a supplier is by actually ordering from them. Once you have settled on a supplier and listed their products on your dropshipping site, you should place a few small orders with the supplier to test how reliable they are.

Making test orders is a great technique for a couple of reasons. First of all, it allows you to gauge how fast the supplier typically delivers orders to clients. Secondly, it also provides you with samples which you can use to determine the quality of the supplier's products. In addition, by ordering from the supplier, you will have placed yourself in the customer's shoes, which will give you a better understanding of what your customers should expect when you choose to work with said supplier.

Of course, you cannot possibly order samples of all the products you intend to sell in your store, but by ordering a few samples, you will have a rough idea of the product quality, the average time a delivery takes and the quality of the packaging used by the supplier.

Advantages of using AliExpress to find suppliers: Finding dropshipping suppliers on AliExpress has a number of advantages. Some of them include:

There a hundreds of millions of products on AliExpress, so the chances of not finding the product you are looking for are quite minimal.

Unlike supplier directories, which might charge you some fees to access their database of suppliers, AliExpress is completely free. This makes it a good option for entrepreneurs who are trying to get their dropshipping business running with minimal costs.

The prices on AliExpress are very competitive, which gives you a nice opportunity to make substantial margins.

New products are added to AliExpress overnight, which allows you take advantage of trends, since you can dropship products that some other suppliers have yet to stock.

AliExpress has built-in customer protection, which means that your chances of getting scammed are relatively low.

Disadvantages of using AliExpress: While AliExpress is a great option for finding dropshipping suppliers and sourcing products, it has some downsides as well. Some of these include:

Unless you are using ePacket shipping, shipping might take a long time, depending on where the product needs to be delivered.

It is not possible to bundle items. For instance, if a customer orders three products you source from different suppliers, you have no way of ensuring that the products arrive together.

Requirements For Working With Dropshipping Suppliers

So far, we have discussed how to find dropshipping suppliers and how to tell great suppliers from fake suppliers. However, before you grab the phone and start reaching out to suppliers, there are a couple of things you need to set in order.

Your business needs to be legal: Before allowing dropshipping merchants to apply for accounts with them, most legitimate suppliers will require the merchants to provide proof that they are legal businesses. A merchant cannot see product prices nor place orders before their accounts get approved. This means that your dropshipping store will have to be legally incorporated before you can start taking advantage of suppliers' wholesale prices. If your aim is to only ask some basic questions, you can do this without having to provide any documentation. However, you cannot really start your business without properly setting up your business. I am going to discuss this in greater detail in Chapter Five.

Understand your position: Suppliers are constantly getting contacted by aspiring dropshipping entrepreneurs with grand plans who ask hundreds of questions and generally take up lots of their time and then leave without ordering anything. This means that, if you are in the process of launching a new dropshipping store, suppliers won't be ready to go out of their way to please you and help you set up your business.

Suppliers will answer your questions and even help you set up a wholesaler account if you are ready for one. However, don't start asking for discounted prices or spend hours on the phone with their representatives before you have even ordered a single thing from them. Doing this will only end up ruining your reputation with them, which will in turn hurt your relationship with the supplier.

Before you start making any special requests, take the time to build up some credibility first. When you discuss your business plans with the supplier, be definitive instead of giving vague assurances. For instance, tell them that you are launching your store on December 1st instead of saying that you are thinking of launching sometime in the near future. If you have had any professional success in the past that would make you appear more credible, let the supplier know about it. The essence of this is to convince the supplier that whatever inconvenience you are causing them by asking for a special request will pay off later once your business starts flourishing.

Be confident in yourself: You need to get confident, pick up the phone, and make the actual call to the supplier. I have seen several aspiring dropshipping entrepreneurs who are unable to make the call to suppliers. They opt for emailing instead. Sure, email works in some cases, but if you want to be able to quickly get whatever information you need and negotiate a good deal for yourself, you should pick up the phone and make that call.

Suppliers are used to having different people call them. They have friendly representatives who will be more than happy to help you and answer your questions, even if you are a newbie entrepreneur. However, to avoid wasting their time and to ensure that you get all the information you need, I would recommend that you write down your questions beforehand. Talking to the representative is a lot easier when you have a pre-written list of questions to ask and of everything you need to know from the supplier.

Chapter Summary

In this chapter, you have learned:

- How to identify "fake" dropshipping wholesalers.
- How to identify good suppliers.
- How to find dropshipping suppliers.
- The requirements for working with dropshipping suppliers.

In the next chapter, you will be taken through the process of setting up your dropshipping business.

Chapter Five: Setting Up Your Dropshipping Business

By this point, you have a clear understanding of dropshipping and how dropshipping orders are fulfilled. You have also selected a suitable niche, decided on the products to carry in your store, and identified the suppliers you are going to work with. Now is the time to move to the actual set up for your dropshipping business. However, before I take you through the process of building your business, there are a few things you need to know.

One of the things I have observed with first-time online entrepreneurs is that most of them make the mistake of assuming that building an online business is an easy process. When it comes to building a successful business, you have to adopt a long-term view of things and have a high level of commitment—

regardless of whether it's a brick-and-mortar store or an online business. Owing to the thousands of glamorous online business success stories littering the internet, most people start an online business with very unrealistic expectations. If your aim is to throw up a website and sit back expecting a six-figure income in two months, you are going to be very disappointed. However, if you start with realistic expectations and a clear understanding of the amount of investment it will take to get you there, you will be less likely to quit when things get tough.

During the early stages of building your dropshipping business, you will have to make a major investment, either in time or money.

Investing Your Time

If it is your first time building a dropshipping business, I will always advise you to invest more time than money. Investing time in this crucial stage of your business will help you learn all the intricacies of how the business operates and gain a deep understanding of your customers and the market, something that will help you make better decisions. On top of that, you are less likely to waste your money on useless operations that are not critical to the success of your business.

It might be challenging to invest a lot of time in your new business, especially if you are working a 9-5 job and want to build your business on the side. However, the beauty of starting a dropshipping business is that it's easier to run on a part-time basis as compared to running a brick-and-mortar business. All you need are a few hours each day or about 10 to 15 hours every week. During these early days, most of your efforts should be focused on marketing your business. As your business starts growing and the money starts flowing in, you can gradually transition into working on it full-time.

The other thing to keep in mind when investing time in your dropshipping business is that in the early days, you may need to put in a lot of effort which might not seem to be bearing a lot of fruit. However, once your store is up and running, it will need significantly less time to maintain it. You will start making more money while doing less work.

Investing Your Money

If it is entirely impossible to dedicate your time to your dropshipping business, it is possible to grow the business by investing a bunch of money in it. However, this is not advisable, and I will always insist that if you can, you should always be out there doing most of the work and getting your hands dirty. Without a hands-on approach to the business, you will only end up wasting your money on useless operations that will not drive the overall success of the business. However, it's important to note that even if you decide to work full-time on your new business, you will still need some capital to launch the business and get operational.

With that out of the way, now we can move on to the actual process of setting up your business.

Register Your Dropshipping Business

Remember, I mentioned that your business has to be legally registered with the proper government agencies before you can start working with dropshipping suppliers. When it comes to registering businesses in the United States, there are three business structures that are commonly used:

Sole proprietorship: This is the simplest structure you can register your business under. It has minimal filings. Your business earnings can be simply reported on your personal taxes. However, this structure offers no liability protection, which means that if your business is sued, your personal assets will also be at risk.

Limited Liability Company (LLC): This structure establishes your business as a separate legal entity, thereby providing more protection for personal assets. While an LLC offers more protection than a sole proprietorship, the protection is not foolproof. An LLC will also come with additional filing requirements.

C Corporation: C Corporations provide the most liability protection. However, registering and incorporating a C Corporation is more expensive compared to the other two. C Corporations are also subject to double taxation.

As a small entrepreneur, you should probably register your business as sole proprietorship or an LLC. Personally, I feel that an LLC is the best choice for a dropshipping business. However,

I would recommend that you consult with a lawyer before making a final decision on this.

After you register your business, you should then apply for an Employer Identification Number (EIN). This number is like the Social Security Number for your company. You will need to provide this number when applying for a wholesaler account with your dropshipping supplier. You will also use it to file your taxes and do other official matters related to your business. You can apply for your business EIN online.

The other thing you need to do is to make sure that you keep your business and personal finances separate. Blending your personal and business finances will cause confusion, make accounting a nightmare and may even get you into trouble with the IRS. The best thing is to ensure that you keep the two totally separate. To do this, you should set up a separate bank account for your business, get a separate credit card and create a separate PayPal account for your business.

Pick Your Sales Channel

With the legal set up of your business out of the way, now you are ready to start selling. Before you can make your first sale, however, you need to decide on the sales channel you will use to sell your products. Where will you place your products so that prospective customers can see them? There are several options available for selling your products. I am going to discuss the three most popular sales channels, which are eBay, Amazon, and your own online store.

Dropshipping On eBay

eBay is the world's largest and most popular online auction site. It has millions of users and offers a good option for getting your dropshipped products in front of prospective buyers.

Advantages Of Dropshipping On eBay

Some of the reasons why eBay is a good option for dropshipping your products include:

Easy to set up: Selling items on eBay is very easy. All you need to do is sign up for an eBay account and you can immediately start listing your products. No hassle about building a store and no long verification process.

Wide reach: Like I mentioned, eBay has millions of users from all around the globe. By listing your products on eBay, you get access to all these people. Your products will be seen by millions of people. Since eBay is a fairly reputable platform, people won't be afraid of buying your products off the platform either.

Less marketing: One of the biggest advantages of dropshipping your products on eBay is that you don't have to worry about the tough task of getting traffic to your products. This is one of the hardest tasks when it comes to building a business. Dropshipping on eBay allows you to take advantage of the traffic on their enormous platform.

Disadvantages Of Dropshipping On eBay

Despite these advantages, there are some downsides to dropshipping your products on eBay. These include:

Listing fees: This is the biggest drawback of using eBay to sell your dropshipped products. Having to pay a 10% or higher fee for the successful sale of your product can significantly drive down your margins. This becomes a huge problem for dropshipping entrepreneurs since the margins are not very large to begin with.

No customization: To list your products on eBay, you will have to use the templates provided by eBay. This means it will be a challenge to create a branded, professional, and value-added listing for your products.

Continuous monitoring ad re-listing: Since eBay is basically built as an auction-style marketplace, the listings on the platform are set to expire after a certain period of time. This means that as a dropshipping merchant, you will need to continuously monitor your products and relist those that have expired. This can be a tedious process as compared to having a static product listing. While there are some tools available to automate this process, it is still a bit hectic.

Customer relationship constraints: eBay is not built to help you build customer relationships. Sure, some customers will buy from you twice or thrice, but there's not much you can do to keep customers coming back to you. Your communication with customers, your branding, and your store design are severely limited on eBay, so building a loyal customer base will be a great challenge.

eBay is not an asset: If you are able to create your own dropshipping store that generates a substantial income and has a loyal customer base, this business is an actual asset that you can sell to someone else. On the contrary, when you dropship your products on eBay, you won't be able to build a lasting brand or a business with any tangible value. If you decide to go out of business, you cannot sell your eBay account.

Dropshipping On Amazon

Amazon is the number one online marketplace in the world, with yearly net sales that run into hundreds of billions of dollars each year. The platform attracts huge traffic, which dropshipping merchants can take advantage of to sell their products. Actually, a huge percentage of the products listed on Amazon are sold by third-party merchants.

Dropshipping your products on Amazon has similar advantages to dropshipping on eBay. Getting started is fairly easy, you get instant access to millions of prospective customers, and you don't have to spend your time and money on marketing and traffic generation. On top of that, Amazon has a program known as Fulfillment by Amazon (FBA), which makes it possible for merchants to complement dropshipped products with their own products while Amazon handles the warehousing, packing, and shipping.

Despite these advantages, Amazon also has its downsides. Just like with eBay, you will have to pay commission fees, which in the 10% - 15% range, which takes a large portion of your profits. Similarly, building long-term customer relationships is next to impossible on Amazon. These online marketplaces are focused on the products and not the sellers, so this is something you will have to deal with. You cannot customize your product listings or in any way influence the customer experience. All this is under Amazon's control. Another huge disadvantage is that Amazon has access to your sales data, which they can use to drive their own agenda. There have been cases where Amazon has been accused of using merchants' sales data to identify well performing niches and strengthen itself in these niches, thereby pushing out the smaller merchants selling through the platform.

Selling In Your Own Online Store

As you have seen above, dropshipping your products on Amazon or eBay is not good for the long-term well-being of your dropshipping business. If you want to avoid the disadvantages associated with dropshipping your products on online marketplaces and build a business that you have great control over, you should build your own online store. This is the method I prefer most, since it allows you to be an independent entrepreneur and build your own brand. Let's take a more detailed look into why you should build your own online store:

Advantages Of Building Your Own Online Store

Full control: With your own online store, you are in control of everything—your branding, your store design, the look and layout of your product listings, everything. This allows you to decide the kind of buying experience you want your customers to have and add value for your customers, which we saw is a key element if you want to succeed in selling products online.

Better income: With your own store, you can charge higher prices because you are able to provide more value for your customers. You do not have to pay any commission or listing fees on your own store either, which means you will earn more profits.

No competition: When you sell your products on online marketplaces like Amazon and eBay, you will have to contend with lots of competitors selling similar products, often at lower prices. Since you cannot differentiate yourself through branding, you will be reduced to competing on price, which is not healthy for any business. On the other hand, when you sell your products on your own store, there are no other sellers to compete with.

Easy design: There are several platforms that make it easy to build your own online store, even if you have no technical skills. They have dozens of templates and allow you to make customizations to suit your preferences. With these platforms, your online store can be up and running in less than a day. Some of these platforms even make it possible for you to manage your business from your smartphone.

Analytics: With your own store, you have access and control over business data, including sales volumes, visitor numbers, visitor sources and demographics, and so much more. You can use this data to measure your business's performance and tweak your strategy to grow your business even further.

You build a real business: Your own ecommerce store is a real business that has its own brand. If you decide to get out of the dropshipping business, you can easily value your online store and sell it.

Disadvantages Of Selling In Your Own Online Store

Traffic generation: When you sell your products on online marketplaces, you can take advantage of the millions of buyers who frequent these sites. However, when you build your own store, no one knows about it, so you will have to embark on an aggressive SEO and marketing campaign to drive traffic to your store. This is not easy. You will have to invest significant amounts of time and money before you can see substantial results. The good thing is, once business picks up, you will need much less effort to keep the business running.

Platforms For Building Your Store

Most people think that building an ecommerce store is a hard task that requires advanced skills in site building, coding, and web design. They are totally wrong. Anyone can build their own online store with plug-and-play platforms that are available online. Here, I will look at two popular platforms that you can use to build your online store. However, before I go into that, you need to know that your online store will always be a work-in-progress. If you decide to wait until you have a perfect website before you launch your store, you might never launch. Do what you can and keep improving as you move on.

While there are several platforms for building online stores, the two most popular platforms are Shopify and WooCommerce.

Shopify: This is simply the best platform when it comes to building a standalone online store. Shopify takes care of all the technical aspects of setting up your ecommerce website and running it, from handling the web-hosting bits to making your site secure and processing credit card payments. By taking care of the technical aspects of your dropshipping business, they allow you to concentrate on marketing and driving traffic to your website. On top of that, they have thousands of apps that you can use to extend the functionalities of your online store.

WooCommerce: This is another powerful toolkit that you can use to build your online store. WooCommerce is an open source platform, which allows you to make whatever modifications and customizations you want on your site. Unlike Shopify, it doesn't exercise any controls over your site's data, which is a big plus. However, WooCommerce is more suitable for small businesses. Managing a big store with WooCommerce can be a bit challenging. Unlike Shopify, WooCommerce is free, though you will need to pay for licenses and buy third-party plugins in order to extend your store's functionality.

Promoting Your Dropshipping Business

Once your dropshipping store goes live and is ready to meet its first customers, now is the time to get it in front of as many prospective customers as you can and attract them so they can become paying customers. This is one of the most challenging parts of starting a dropshipping business. However, without promoting your business, your chances of success are next to zero. Luckily, if you commit yourself and do it right, you will enjoy massive results.

There are several channels you can use to promote your dropshipping business. While each business has a different channel that works best for it, I am going to look at five proven methods you can use to promote your online store. You don't have to use all of them. Focus on the methods that suit you best.

Social Media Marketing (SMM)

Social media marketing is the use of social media sites to create brand awareness, create customer relationships, gain traffic, and drive sales. These can be done on major social media platforms such as Facebook, Twitter, Instagram, Pinterest, Google+, LinkedIn, and YouTube, as well as on online forums and blogs. While many people see social media as nothing more than a social tool, it is something that you can leverage to drive sales for your dropshipping business. When creating a social media marketing campaign for your business, you should avoid trying to market your business on every social media platform. While it might seem like a good strategy to gain maximum reach, it will be overwhelming for you and you will end up achieving dismal results on each of these sites. What you should do is identify two to three social media platforms that will deliver maximum results and dedicate all your focus to them. All in all, social media is a great tool for marketing your dropshipping business. Avoid social media marketing at your own risk.

Facebook Ads

While this is an off-shoot of social media marketing, it deserves its own mention because of its effectiveness as an online marketing tool. Facebook is the largest and the most popular social marketing platform in the world. The platform has over 1.71 billion monthly active users, which makes it the ideal place to advertise your dropshipping business. However, the effectiveness of Facebook as a marketing tool goes beyond the numbers. Unlike most advertising platforms which serve ads on query-based data, Facebook serves its ads based on contextual data. With query-based data, the advertising platform shows adverts that are relevant to what users are searching for on the internet. A good example of a query-based advertising platform is Google Adwords.

In contrast, platforms that serve advertisements based on contextual data allow advertisers to choose the demographics of the people they want to see their advertisements based on context. This makes it easier for you to target a specific audience. Are your products geared toward 25-year-old men living in California who have an obsession with sport bikes? You can target this exact group with Facebook ads. Facebook advertisements allow you to choose you audience based on factors like age, geographical location, interests, behavior, job position, and so much more. This means that Facebook advertisements are more relevant and are more likely to drive conversions.

To make your Facebook advertising campaign more effective, you should first come up with a clear objective for the campaign. Is your aim to create awareness for your brand? Is it to drive people to your dropshipping store? Is it to increase your sales? Having a clear objective will help you craft an effective marketing campaign. On top of that, Facebook provides you with a variety of options that make it easier for you to achieve your marketing objectives.

The other things you should keep in mind in order to create a relevant Facebook advertisement is to ensure that you use persuasive, relevant, and actionable copy, use relevant and attention-grabbing images, and use a clear and concise Call to Action (CTA).

Search Engine Optimization (SEO)

Search Engine Optimization is the process of finetuning your site in order to capture traffic from search engines like Google. In other words, it is the process of ensuring that your dropshipping business can be found on search engines. SEO is a broad topic and consists of many elements. However, to make it simpler to understand, SEO can be broken down into the steps. The first one is defining the keywords that you want your site to rank for. This means that when people search for these keywords, they should be able to find your site on the first page of Google. You will have to do extensive keyword research to find appropriate keywords that you want to rank for. The second step is optimizing your site for the keywords you defined in step one. Step three is building backlinks to your dropshipping store. Having many backlinks on your dropshipping store gives Google's algorithms the perception that your site is an authoritative one, which in turn leads to a higher ranking on the search engine results pages.

By properly utilizing SEO tactics, your dropshipping store will rank higher on search engines, which means that you will have more people finding your store, visiting it, and buying your products. SEO allows you to direct traffic to your dropshipping store without having to pay for it.

While performing proper SEO to ensure your store ranks high on search results is not a necessarily easy task, it is still doable.

Defining the keywords you want to rank for and optimizing your store for these keywords is the easy part. The hard part is trying to outrank your competitors for the same keywords, especially when your store is still relatively new and has yet to build some authority. This is where backlinks come in handy. Backlinks from high-quality sources will help raise your store's authority.

SEO is something you want to ensure you are doing right. According to data by Custora, organic search traffic drives about 26% of all orders on ecommerce stores. By improving your site's SEO, you can increase your sales by up to 26% percent. One thing you should keep in mind is that you won't see immediate results with SEO. Initially, you will hardly see any results, but in the long run, you will reap exponential rewards.

Email Marketing

Email is one of the most cost-effective tools you can use to market your dropshipping business and gain customer engagement. Email generates high-quality leads and high-quality conversions, which is why it has a return on investment (ROI) of 44%. If you do it right, you will see massive results. Email is so effective because people share their contact details voluntarily, which is a sure-fire sign that they are interested in your products. Email marketing also allows you to accumulate your prospect's personal data, which you can use in further interactions. By providing quality content through email, you can create more demand for your products.

To run an effective email marketing campaign, you should have an attractive lead magnet for your site. As a dropshipping business, your lead magnet can be a loyalty program that provides subscribers with exclusive discounts. You should have a well-designed email template and ensure that your regularly communicate with your subscribers. However, this does not mean constantly spamming them with sales emails. This will only lead to people opting out of your email list. Instead, you should always strive to provide value through your email newsletters.

Video Marketing

The greatest thing about video marketing is that it makes it possible for you to create an instant connection with your audience. Posts with videos lead to more time spent on your site and increased engagement. Search engine algorithms also tend to give more importance to videos, which means that using videos will improve your ranking, increase your conversions, and have greater results on your brand awareness campaign.

The most effective way of using videos to promote your dropshipping business is to create video reviews of the products you sell in your store. These can range from amateur reviews by previous customers to professional and detailed reviews of a product's features, performance, and benefits. If you decide on using video marketing to promote your store, create a YouTube channel that matches your store design, provide information about your business on the channel, and make sure that your channel is also optimized for search engines.

Chapter Summary

In this chapter, we have covered:

- How to register your dropshipping business.
- How to pick your sales channel.
- Suitable platforms for building your own online dropshipping store.
- How to promote your dropshipping business.

In the next chapter, you are going to learn about various aspects of running your dropshipping business.

Chapter Six: Running Your Dropshipping Business

If it's your first time running a dropshipping business, the early days can be quite hectic. The information in this chapter will make the whole process easier for you and save you lots of time and headaches. Before we get started, you should note that things are going to get messy sometimes. There are issues you will have to deal with every now and then. By accepting this from the beginning, it will be easier to deal with them and avoid frustration. In addition, you should keep everything as simple as you can. Dropshipping is a complex operation, so the simpler you can keep things, the better for you and your customers.

With that out of the way, let's look at how to deal with various aspects of your dropshipping business.

Managing Inventory

One of the most challenging aspects of running a dropshipping business is managing the status of your inventory, especially when you source your products from multiple suppliers. Without proper inventory management, many customers will find themselves placing orders for out-of-stock products, which is not the way to build a loyal customer base. Managing inventory properly and keeping the number of out-of-stock items at a minimum is a complex process, especially when your suppliers do not offer real-time data feeds. However, you can use the following tips to minimize the chances of your customers ordering out-of-stock products:

Have multiple suppliers: It is always a good idea to have multiple suppliers who have overlapping inventories. This way, if a product is out of stock with supplier A, you can still get it from supplier B or C. This also keeps you cushioned in case one supplier goes out of business or decides to raise their prices. You will hardly find any two suppliers with identical inventories, but suppliers operating in the same niche will often have overlapping inventories—particularly the best-selling items, which are what you should be interested in.

Choose your products wisely: This is an extension of the above point. By focusing on best-selling items, you can be sure that several suppliers in that niche will have these products in stock.

Take advantage of generics: In some cases, different suppliers might have two slightly different items which can be interchanged for each other. This is particularly suitable for small accessories and add-ons. If you have two suppliers that carry interchangeable products, list the product with a generic product description. This way, you can fulfill the order from either of the two suppliers. However, when doing this, you should be careful about substituting products from established brand names.

Check product availability: Don't list a product on your store just because a supplier has it listed on their website. Before listing the item on your store, call the supplier to determine that the product is actually in stock. Also find out if the supplier stocks the product on a regular basis.

How to deal with out-of-stock orders: Even with the best inventory management, you will still have instances when ordered products will be out of stock. Instead of cancelling the order, offer the customer a complimentary upgrade to a better product.

This ensures you get the sale and can help turn them into a loyal customer.

Order Fulfillment

As I already noted, you should work with multiple suppliers for your dropshipping business. However, this presents another challenge. If a customer orders a product that is stocked by two suppliers, which supplier should you choose to fulfill the order? There are several ways of choosing the best supplier to fulfill an order:

Use a preferred supplier: If one of your suppliers has a great product selection, offers superior service, and has fast delivery times, you can opt to use that supplier for all your orders by default. This makes processing orders a breeze for you. You can have your store automatically forward all confirmed orders to this supplier's email address. However, you need to ensure that this supplier stocks most of the items in your store.

Select suppliers by location: If you have multiple suppliers stocking the product ordered by your customer, you could choose to forward the order to the supplier located closest to your customer. This leads to faster delivery and saves on shipping costs.

Select suppliers by availability: If your inventory is spread out across several suppliers, you will have to pick the supplier that has the ordered product in stock. With this option, you will have to forward the orders manually. However, there are services that allow you to automate this process if your supplier provides an automated data feed.

Select suppliers based on price: While this sounds like a great option in theory, it is quite complex. Automatically determining the cheapest supplier is complicated since you have to take into account factors like pricing, real-time shipping fees, and potential drop fees. Implementing an automated system to handle this can be challenging.

There is no perfect method for choosing the best supplier to fulfill an order. You should make the decision based on your suppliers, you store, and personal preferences.

Dealing With Botched Orders

When running a dropshipping business, it is inevitable that sometimes your suppliers will make fulfillment errors. The supplier might ship the wrong item or even ship nothing at all. In such cases, the first thing you should do is own the mistake. Never put the blame on your supplier. The customer is not even aware that you are dropshipping their order, so doing this will only cause confusion. Instead, own the mistake, apologize to the customer, and let them know you are working to fix the problem. You should then make it up to the customer depending on the nature of the error. For instance, you might opt to refund the shipping fee or offer an upgrade if the customer needs you to ship out a new item.

While it is important for you to own the mistake, you don't have to pay for it. Instead, follow up with the supplier and have them pay for their own errors, such as paying the shipping costs for the return and shipping of the new product.

While it is inevitable for suppliers to make a mistake or two, you should quit working with suppliers who habitually botch orders, since this will end up ruining your business's reputation.

Dealing With Security And Fraud Issues

Storing Customers' Financial Information

While storing your customers' financial information makes it convenient for your customers to reorder from your store, it is usually not worth the hassle, especially if you are hosting your own site. You have to comply with all Payment Card Industry (PCI) rules, which is a complex and expensive process. You will also be liable if your site gets hacked and customer information is stolen.

To avoid all these problems, you should not store customer financial information. If you are using a self-hosted shopping cart, you should make sure that the "store card information" feature is disabled. However, if you are using ecommerce platforms like Shopify, you do not have to worry about this.

Dealing With Fraudulent Orders

When running an ecommerce business, the risk of fraudulent orders is ever present. While this might be quite scary at first, you can prevent fraud-related losses by exercising a bit of caution and common sense. One of the most common and popular measures you can take to prevent fraud on your store is to adopt the

Address Verification System. With this feature, the transaction only gets approved when the customer enters the address associated with their credit card. This makes it impossible for thieves to make purchases with the credit card number only. Chances of fraudulent orders passing the AVS check are very slim.

With most fraudulent ecommerce orders, the billing address is usually different from the shipping address. However, this presents a challenging situation. By not allowing customers to ship orders to an address that is different from their billing address, you could lose out on genuine orders. On the other hand, by allowing this, you put your store at risk of fraudulent orders. You will be liable in the event that fraudulent orders are placed on your site.

There are a number of signs you can use to spot a potentially fraudulent order. The billing and shipping addresses are usually different on more than 95% of all fraudulent orders. Different names on the shipping and billing address are another sign of a potentially fraudulent order. However, it could be a legitimate gift purchase. If the email address looks unusual, there is a high chance of the order being fraudulent. Fraudsters also choose the fastest—and usually the most expensive—delivery method. They want to minimize the time you have to catch them. They also do not care about the expense since the card is not theirs. While any of these signs is not a surefire way of detecting fraud, if you notice two or three of these red flags, you should be cautious.

If you notice a fraudulent order, call the customer to confirm the order. If they sound confused or if you find a dead line, simply cancel the order and issue a refund.

Chargebacks

Chargebacks occur when a customer contacts their bank or credit card company with a claim against a charge made by you. In this situation, your payment processor deducts the amount in dispute from your account until you can prove that you indeed delivered a good or service to the customer. If you cannot prove this, you lose the deducted amount and pay a $25 chargeback processing fee. If you accrue too many chargebacks, your merchant account might end up being terminated.

Chargebacks are usually a result of fraud, though legitimate customers might also claim a chargeback if they don't recognize your business, if they forgot about the purchase, or if they are not satisfied with the product they received.

When you are hit with a chargeback, you should provide documentation about the order, as well as the shipping invoice. If the transaction was legitimate, you have a good chance of recovering your money. However, if the chargeback is associated with an order that has different billing and shipping addresses, your chances of recovering the funds are next to zero.

Dealing With Returns

Before you come up with a return policy for your dropshipping store, you should first have a clear understanding of your suppliers' return policies. One supplier's return policy might force you to rethink your entire return policy. Some factors that might affect your return policy include:

Restocking fees: Some suppliers may require you to pay a restocking fee for returned items. Even if your supplier has a restocking fee, it is not advisable to incorporate such fees in your return policy. Doing so might cost you customers in the long run. It is much better to foot the restocking fees and chalk it up to brand building and customer relationship expenses.

Defective items: Receiving a defective item can be very irritating for your customers. Having to pay shipping fees to return it is even worse. Unfortunately, most dropshipping suppliers do not cover the shipping costs for returning defective items. Since they did not manufacture the products, they don't want to take liability for any defects. However, if you want to build a good reputation for your dropshipping business, always give your customers a refund for any expenses they incur while returning a defective item.

In cases where the defective item is fairly inexpensive, it might be a better idea to just ship a new product to the customer without having them return the defective one. Doing this is sometimes more cost effective. It will probably also pleasantly surprise your customer, which might end up landing you a lifetime customer. Even though suppliers don't cover the shipping costs of returning a defective product, they might have no problem with paying the shipping costs to send the replacement to the customer.

However, if the customer wants a refund for the defective product, it is not unreasonable to ask them to foot the costs of returning the product.

Dealing With Shipping Issues

Calculation of shipping rates is another challenging task you will encounter when running a dropshipping business. When you have to ship different products from different locations, automatically calculating the shipping fees will be a bit complicated. To make this task easier for you, there are three shipping rate models that you can use. The first one is the real-time rate model, where your shopping cart gives a real-time shipping quote based on the weight of ordered items and the shipping destination. While this method is very accurate, it becomes ineffective when products have to be shipped from different locations. The second model is the per-type rate, where you charge a flat rate shipping fee depending on the type of product ordered. Lastly, you can apply a flat-rate shipping model, where all orders are shipped at the same rate regardless of type.

As with other aspects of running a dropshipping business, I emphasize simplicity over perfection when it comes to your preferred shipping rate model. Choose something that works and then tweak it as your business grows instead of obsessing over developing a perfect model when you have yet to make a single sale.

Customer Support

As your business grows, you will have to come up with an effective way of handling your customers' issues. While you can use an Excel spreadsheet to manage customer requests and emails, it will quickly become overwhelming. My recommendation for managing your store's customer support is to implement a helpdesk. A helpdesk is a software that makes it easy for you to manage correspondence with your customers from one centralized location. There are several helpdesk options you can use. Some of the most popular include Help Scout, Zendesk, Desk, and Kayako.

Alternatively, you can offer phone support. This is a great and professional way of providing real-time customer support. However, offering phone support is very expensive. Before you opt for phone support, you should evaluate your dropshipping business and the kind of products you sell to see if it's worth it. For instance, if you sell $1,000 jewelry, customers might want to talk to a sales representative before placing their orders. In this case, you need to offer phone support. However, if you sell $20 - $50 accessories, customers will comfortably buy without having to talk to anyone, and therefore phone support may not be really necessary.

However, one thing you should keep in mind is that regardless of the customer support method you use, you should always be ready to get on the phone to resolve any issues your customers may have after placing an order.

Chapter Summary

In this chapter, you have learned:

- How to deal with inventory management.
- How to choose the best supplier to fulfill an order.
- How to deal with botched orders.
- How to deal with security and fraud issues.
- How to deal with chargebacks.
- How to deal with returns.
- How to deal with shipping issues.
- How to provide customer support.

Conclusion

Thanks again for taking the time to purchase this book!

You should now have a good understanding of dropshipping, and be able to start and grow a successful dropshipping business.

If you enjoyed this book, please take the time to leave me a review on Amazon. I appreciate your honest feedback, and it really helps me to continue producing high quality books.

About The Author

31-year-old Anthony Parker is a self-made Internet entrepreneur, investor & author.

Anthony first entered the world of Online Business in 2014 with the creation of his first dropshipping store, since then Anthony has created and sold 3 other dropshipping stores and has since ventured out into Amazon FBA and Affiliate Marketing with the goal of creating long-term highly profitable passive income streams.

Anthony latest venture is to share his knowledge and passion on the world of Online Business with the goal of making seemingly complex and intimidating topics simple and easy-to-read with the hope of encouraging others to become internet entrepreneurs

Printed in Great Britain
by Amazon